Wallace & Gromit™
in
A Grand Day Out™

Teacher's Book

Lorena Roberts

OXFORD
UNIVERSITY PRESS

OXFORD
UNIVERSITY PRESS

Great Clarendon Street, Oxford OX2 6DP

Oxford University Press is a department of the University of Oxford.
It furthers the University's objective of excellence in research, scholarship,
and education by publishing worldwide in

Oxford New York

Auckland Cape Town Dar es Salaam Hong Kong Karachi
Kuala Lumpur Madrid Melbourne Mexico City Nairobi
New Delhi Shanghai Taipei Toronto

With offices in

Argentina Austria Brazil Chile Czech Republic France Greece
Guatemala Hungary Italy Japan Poland Portugal Singapore
South Korea Switzerland Thailand Turkey Ukraine Vietnam

OXFORD and OXFORD ENGLISH are registered trade marks of
Oxford University Press in the UK and in certain other countries

ISBN : 978 0 19 459245 1   Student's Book
ISBN : 978 0 19 459246 8   Teacher's Book
ISBN : 978 0 19 459247 5   VHS PAL Video Cassette
ISBN : 978 0 19 459249 9   VHS SECAM Video Cassette
ISBN : 978 0 19 459248 2   VHS NTSC Video Cassette
ISBN : 978 0 19 459238 3   DVD

Printed in China

ACKNOWLEDGEMENTS
The publisher would like to thank Aardman Animations Ltd. for their
co-operation and assistance.

Contents

To the teacher

A GRAND DAY OUT STUDENT'S BOOK

A Grand Day Out has been broken down into six short episodes. For each episode the Student's Book contains the following material:

Watching the video

Four pages of activities for classroom exploitation. We recommend allowing a double lesson (90 – 100 minutes) to benefit fully from the video and the suggested activities.

The activities are based around the following viewing stages:

1 Viewing of the complete episode

At this level show the students the whole episode before breaking it down for more detailed language work. This encourages students to watch and listen in order to understand in general what is happening and provides a context for the activities which follow.

2 Viewing the episode in sections

Each of the episodes is divided into two sections. Breaking the episodes down in this way makes understanding of the story easier and allows for more thorough exploitation of the language.

3 Watching the whole episode again

It's very important to let students watch the whole episode again, after they have completed the activities and practised the language. As well as being enjoyable, it enables the students to appreciate how much more they can now understand.

For each of the viewing stages there are various activities with different aims and objectives as follows:

Before you watch activities

These pre-viewing tasks have been designed to do one or more of the following:

*   pre-teach key vocabulary,
*   introduce a key structure,
*   set the scene.

While you watch activities

These tasks include:

*   observational activities in which students are asked to watch and / or listen for specific details, or
*   checking activities in which students watch in order to check their answers to a previously completed exercise.

After you watch activities

By this stage, students should be fairly familiar with the sequence. These tasks encourage students to focus on a variety of aspects such as:

*   idiomatic expressions,
*   sequencing and narrating events,
*   comprehension,
*   language review.

Practice

There are two pages of practice activities at the end of each episode. These activities aim to provide further practice and extension of the key vocabulary and structures. This is usually done via oral pairwork activities in which students practise modelled dialogues, play pairwork games, learn simple chants, etc.

These activities can be completed without access to video equipment.

Transcripts

The transcripts have been provided as reference to use **after** the lesson. Students often like to read the transcripts, make notes and add translations. This is usually done at home and should not be discouraged as any extra work can only be advantageous. However, we would advise teachers not to use the transcripts before any of the viewing stages, but rather as a review, particularly with higher levels.

Picture dictionary

At the end of the Student's Book is a list of 55 words from the story with pictures to illustrate their meaning.

TEACHING WITH VIDEO: Some techniques

Silent viewing activities

This means turning off the sound on the TV and watching the visuals on their own. The best way to do this is to use the MUTE control. This technique can be used either for **prediction** or **reproduction**.

a Prediction

Students view for the first time with no sound and guess or predict what is happening and what is being said using only visual clues.

b Reproduction

This type of activity gets the students to reproduce either the dialogue or the narrative, having already seen and heard the sequence.

It is also be more effective when the class have done some preparatory work on particular expressions, structures, pronunciation or narrative techniques.

c Random sound down (Cloze listening)

This is similar to a 'gapped' dialogue in which students fill in the spaces. Turn the sound off at random intervals asking the students to fill in the missing dialogue or narrative.

Sound only activities

This is where the students hear the dialogue and narration without any pictures. You can do this in a number of ways: by using the brightness controls on the TV, by unplugging the picture connectors, or simply by placing something over or in front of the television set to obscure the picture.

Students can then use the sound alone either to predict what they think is happening or, having seen and heard the sequence before, they can use the dialogue to help them remember what the characters are doing.

Freeze framing (still picture) activities

Freeze framing means stopping the picture using the FREEZE FRAME, STILL or PAUSE control.

a Prediction

If students are viewing a sequence for the first time, you can freeze the frame and ask them to predict what's going to happen or what a character is going to say next.

b Reproduction

Freeze frame at intervals and ask the class to tell you what has just happened.

c Background detail

There is a great deal of background detail which can easily be missed in a video sequence. Using FREEZE FRAME is a useful way of exploring a video sequence in more depth, picking out background events, scenery, and information about British life and culture.

d Thoughts and emotions

Video gives us an additional dimention of information from the characters' body language, facial expressions, gesture, stance, reaction and response. Use FREEZE FRAME to talk about a character's feelings or reactions at a given moment. Gromit is wonderfully expressive without ever saying a word. Encourage students to imagine what he or other characters are thinking.

Paired viewing activities

Paired viewing activities require more planning and preparation but the results are often well worth the extra effort.

a Description

One student (A) in each pair turns their back to the screen or monitor while the video is played silently. The other student (B) describes what he or she can see. Both students then watch the sequence again with sound and compare it with A's description of the events. Swap roles with a different sequence so that each partner has the opportunity to be both the speaker and the listener.

b Narration

Send half of the class out of the room while the other half watches the video. Those who left the room are then paired up with a student who watched the video and can now describe what happened. If this involves watching the end of a sequence, those who left the room could be asked to write a series of questions based on their own predictions about what they think is going to happen.

c Split class: Description / Narration

Half the class watch a section of the video with sound only. The other half of the class watch the same section with picture only. The students then work together in pairs so that in each pair one student has only seen the section and the other has only heard it. Together they try to retell what happened.

YOUNG LEARNERS

Even very young children with little experience of English can enjoy and learn from the adventures of Wallace and Gromit in *A Grand Day Out*™. It has been proven that exposing children to natural English at an early age improves their language performance in later years, particularly in areas of comprehension and pronunciation. Video is the ideal means of doing this because the visual and language content is so rich.

However, the approach needed to exploit the video most effectively needs to be adapted, and the teaching aims refined. The focus with young learners should be very much on the general rather than the specific, i.e. on the story itself and the more general themes related to it, as opposed to more detailed comprehension and language exploitation.

Teaching younger children favours a globalized approach which draws on children's experiences in all areas of learning across the curriculum. Children learn best when their learning is holistic, rather than compartmentalised into subject areas. The teaching of English should therefore include other areas of learning such as personal and emotional development, communication and expression, and physical and social development. Material such as *A Grand Day Out*™ enables you to do this by drawing on the strong narrative aspect, the visual detail and the sheer appeal of the characters. It offers a springboard into a large number of related topics, appropriate to children, which you can then develop and exploit further in the classroom, e.g.:

- Holidays
- Numbers and counting
- Colours
- Countries
- Food and drink
- Furniture and household objects
- Animals and animal sounds
- Transport, machines and tools

Pre-viewing

With all language learners, and particularly with children, it is important to spend some time preparing the children for the video sequence they are going to watch so that they are not coming to it 'cold'. A short time spent doing a few short pre-viewing activities will increase the children's attention and help their comprehension. This teaching phase usually involves one or more of the following:

a Setting the scene

Discuss with the children what they know about the story so far, the characters, and the setting. At this stage you might want to pre-teach any key vocabulary that will help the children to understand the video sequence they are going to watch.

b Predicting what is going to happen

Encourage the children to draw on their own experiences and what they know about the video already to predict what is going to happen. This is another way of motivating the children to watch attentively and focuses their attention on a chosen aspect of the video sequence.

Watching the video

Make sure the children have a real reason for watching: a specific task that they have to do which will focus their attention. This can be very simple such as a general question about the sequence,

perhaps related to their own predictions, or a specific detail that they must look out for, e.g. where something is located, the colour of a particular object, etc.

Post-viewing activities

With young learners this is where most of the learning will take place. Having used the video sequence to set the scene, to introduce some vocabulary or a simple structure, and to provide the context for the lesson, the children will now be motivated to use the theme or the language in more child-based, cross-curricular activities. These can be one, or a number of, the following activity types:

a Total physical response (TPR)

Children are not very good at sitting still for long periods of time. Using movement helps to make the language more 'real' and more memorable. You can use TPR in a number of ways, e.g.:

- Children pretend to be Wallace and Gromit using movement and mime to 'role-play' short sequences on the video.
- Use observation and facial expressions to discuss and imitate how characters on the video are feeling and their relationship with one another.
- Use mime to practise specific language presented via the video, e.g. children can practise some of the steps Wallace and Gromit go through in building the spaceship in Episode 2: hammering, drilling, welding, painting, etc.; mime is also an effective way to practise and reinforce the prepositions in Episode 3; children can also pretend to be a spaceship counting down and 'blasting off' in Episode 3.

b Art and craft activities

Children use art and craft activities to explore colour, shape and texture via drawing, painting, collage, model making, etc. These activities can be language based, i.e. using language specifically related to the video sequence or they can be topic based, i.e using the context but with more open language aims.

c Language based art activities

Children draw and label pictures. For example, in Episode 1, children can draw a picture of Wallace's sitting-room and label all the objects on Student's Book page 7.

In Episode 5, children draw and label the parts of the Moon machine – or design and label their own machine.

d Picture / colour dictation

Give simple instructions to the children using language related to one or more units, e.g. colours in Episode 2 and household objects / furniture in Episode 1:

Draw a tray. Colour the tray red.

Draw a book on the tray. Colour the book blue.

Draw a cup and saucer on the tray. Colour the cup pink and the saucer grey.

e Topic based craft activities

- Make masks of Wallace and Gromit that the children can use to act out simple exchanges between the two characters.
- Use boxes, cardboard tubes, etc. and paint to make Wallace's spaceship or a Moon machine.
- Use pictures from old books and magazines to make a collage of furniture or foods and drinks, etc.
- Use different textured materials and crescent shapes to create different Moon surfaces.
- Make Wallace a 'lunch box' for his cheese and crackers.
- Design (and write) a postcard from the Moon.

Personalization

Wherever possible, transfer the context and the language to the children's own situation, experience or imagination, e.g.:

- In Episode 1 encourage the children to talk, draw, or write about their own holidays. Alternatively, encourage their self expression and imagination by asking them why (or why not) they would like to go to the Moon on holiday. What would be their dream holiday and why? In instances such as these you may need to revert to the children's own language.
- In Episode 2 the children can talk about their favourite colours, the colours of their clothes or things in the classroom.
- In Episode 4 discuss card games the children play, the foods they would take on a picnic to the Moon, etc.

BACKGROUND NOTES

A Grand Day Out™ was originally written by Nick Park for native speakers of English and has been specially adapted for ELT by Peter Viney and Karen Viney. Other videos starring Wallace and Gromit are the OSCAR®-winning films *The Wrong Trousers*™ and *A Close Shave*™. These, too, have been adapted for ELT by Peter Viney and Karen Viney and published by Oxford University Press.

Cultural notes

The Wallace and Gromit stories are all set in a small industrial town in the north of England, a setting very common to the world of British soap operas. Wallace's redbrick house is about one hundred years old, and this kind of house can be found in any English town. The décor and the furniture, however, are deliberately very similar to that found in urban Britain in the 1950s and 1960s.

Pronunciation

Until recently, British English teaching was dominated by an accent called 'RP' or 'Received Pronunciation' which was the standard English of the BBC, the universities and government, and much of ELT audio material is still produced using RP. However, it was felt that it was important to retain the Northern accents which are an integral part of the style and charm of the Wallace and Gromit stories.

Both voices on the video have Northern accents. Wallace has a Yorkshire accent. He is played in both the original version and in this ELT adaptation by Peter Sallis, an actor famous for his portrayal of a Yorkshireman in a long-running British TV comedy *The Last of the Summer Wine*. The story is narrated by Stephen Tompkinson, who speaks in a Lancashire accent, Lancashire being on the opposite side of the Pennine Hills from Yorkshire.

Northern vowel sounds in words like *bath*, *laugh*, *castle* and *can't* have the same short 'a' as in American English. In 'RP' they would sound like '~~barth~~' and '~~carn't~~'.

Age and language level

The Wallace and Gromit films are enormously popular with audiences of all ages, so, although this particular video is aimed at beginner level, the Student's Book can be used with students who are older and at a higher level. The visuals, music and sound effects are identical to the original version. However, in this ELT adaptation the language level has been greatly simplified and a narrator has been added.

The activities in the Student's Book are aimed at beginner level, although some previous knowledge of English is required. With higher levels, however, the video can be used very effectively for revision purposes, and the teaching notes which follow offer numerous suggestions for ways in which the language and the Student's Book activities can be extended. Many of the techniques in 'Teaching with video' above can be exploited with more fluent learners.

Meet Wallace and Gromit

Before you watch the video, spend some time introducing the characters and discussing the background to the series.

> **Lower levels**
> With lower levels or younger students, don't insist on the use of English in response to your questions if it prevents them expressing themselves. The primary aim of this stage is to stimulate the class's interest in the video and to encourage students to exchange ideas and share what they already know about the characters and the series.

Hold up the video case or the Student's Book so that the class can see the picture on the cover. Ask *Who's this?* Then encourage the class to tell you anything they know about the characters. Help the discussion along by asking questions, e.g.

How do you know these characters?

What films are they in?

Are the films in English or in your own language?

Do you like the films? Why?

Where do Wallace and Gromit live?

In England? America? Australia?

In an apartment? In a house? In a caravan?

Can you tell me anything about Wallace?

How old is he?

Who does he live with?

What does he like eating / drinking?

What does he like doing?

Possible answers include:

Films starring Wallace and Gromit are: *A Grand Day Out*™, *The Wrong Trousers*™ and *A Close Shave*™.

Wallace and Gromit live in a house in England.
Wallace is in his 40s or 50s.
He lives with his dog, Gromit.
He likes drinking tea, and he eats lots of cheese and crackers.
He likes inventing and building machines.

Generally encourage the students to talk as freely as possible about what they know in relation to the characters. If the class do not know or remember many details, encourage them to invent / predict the answers. They can then compare their suggestions with the video later.

> **With higher levels**
> Divide the class into groups and give each group a sheet of paper on which they can write down anything they know about Wallace and Gromit – the films or the characters. If there are only a few students who have seen the films, share them among the groups so that they can tell the others what they know. Those who haven't seen the films should ask questions to those that have and take notes.

After a general class discussion, read the sentences on the Contents page with the class. If you have pictures of other fictional characters, or famous people your students know, ask the class to make similar sentences about them using:

His / Her name is ...

He / She lives in / with ...

Then ask students around the class *What about you? Where do you live? Who do you live with?* The students can then complete the sentences on the Contents page.

Episode 1

Holiday plans

Before you watch the video

1 Ask and answer.

Use the pictures on Student's Book page 4 to teach the vocabulary for different holiday types and to set the scene for the first episode. Point to each picture in turn and read the labels. Ask the class *What's Gromit's favourite holiday?* See if they can find the answer in the speech bubbles at the top of the page. Invite two students to 'be' Wallace and Gromit and read the speech bubbles. Then invite students to ask their classmates the same question.

> **Older students at higher levels**
> Brainstorm other holiday types, e.g. *a cruise, a sailing holiday, an adventure holiday, a touring holiday, a cycling holiday.* Divide the class into groups and allocate each group a different holiday. Explain that they are travel agents and that each group has to try to sell you their holiday. Give the class some time to prepare their sales pitch, then invite volunteers from each group to stand up and sell you their holiday.

Watching the video

Before playing the video ask the class: *Where do Wallace and Gromit decide to go on holiday?* Higher level students could also be asked to explain why.

Note: *Camping* is a very popular form of holiday in Britain with young people and families especially – despite the unreliable weather!

The way Wallace is shown on the beach is a very traditional image of a man enjoying a seaside holiday in Britain, i.e. sitting on a folding chair (*deck-chair*) with his shirt and tie still on, his trousers rolled up and a handkerchief, knotted at each corner, on his head. It is extremely rare nowadays to see such a comically outdated sight on the beach.

Watch all of episode one.

Tell the class to watch all of episode one straight through and see if they can answer your question: *Wallace and Gromit decide to go to the Moon.* Higher levels might add: *Because they have no more cheese in the house, and Wallace thinks the Moon is made of cheese!*

Note: Traditionally, especially in children's stories, the Moon is often shown as a huge cheese because of its round shape, and the fact that its craters resemble the holes found in many well-known cheeses.

Encourage the class to watch and enjoy the first episode without worrying about how much language they can understand. There will be a lot they will get simply from the pictures.

After you watch

2 Tick (✔) the answer.

Tell the class to look at the pictures in the Student's Book and answer the questions. In pairs, the students can then compare answers before checking as a class.

Answers

1 Gromit
2 Gromit
3 Wallace
4 Wallace
5 Wallace

8

Note: British people often call their dogs 'boy' or 'girl'. People say 'Here, boy!' to their dogs. Wallace refers to Gromit as 'lad', e.g. *Wake up, Gromit, lad*. 'Lad' is a common expression in the north of England. It means 'boy' and you can say it to a pet or a boy.

Note: The British are famous around the world for drinking tea! In true British fashion Wallace resorts to a cup of tea whenever there is a problem to solve. Increasingly the British are becoming a more European 'coffee-drinking' nation. However, tea, in the form of herbal tea or mint tea, is becoming popular as a healthier alternative.

SECTION ONE 00.00 TO 00.59

Before you watch

1 Write answers.

Before watching section one, ask the class to try to remember who is sitting in each of the two chairs. You could do a quick survey around the class.

Watch section one.

Confirm students' answers about which of the characters is sitting in each of the chairs. They can then write the sentences.

Answers

Gromit is sitting here (in the spotty chair).
Wallace is sitting here (in the check chair).

After you watch

2 Can you repeat?

Say each line for the class to repeat after you. Pay particular attention to rhythm and intonation. If necessary, repeat section one again and listen to how Wallace says each of the phrases.

> **Older students**
> Invite older students to make up similar chants using other foods or drinks, and ending with the line *Let's have a …*
> e.g.
> *lemonade*
> *glass of lemonade*
> *cold glass of lemonade*
> *a nice cold glass of lemonade*
> *Let's have a nice cold glass of lemonade.*

SECTION TWO 01.00 TO THE END

Before you watch

1 Label the picture.

Read aloud the words in the box. Tell the class to repeat the words after you. Do this chorally, then individually around the class. Tell the students to work in pairs to match each word to one of the objects in the picture. Don't give the answers yet.

Watch section two.

Students can check their answers to activity 1

Answers

teapot		tray
	cracker	
	saucer	
cup		plate

After you watch

2 Complete Wallace's sentences.

Students can complete the sentences orally or in writing using the pictures in the Student's Book as clues.

Answers

No cheese in the fridge!
Let's go to a place with cheese.
The Moon's made of cheese.

3 What countries does Wallace say? Tick (✔) the boxes.

Read the names of the countries aloud with the class, paying particular attention to pronunciation. Write the names on the board and underline the stressed syllables: America, England, France, Brazil, Italy, Japan, Spain, Turkey. Ask the class if they can remember the countries Wallace says. If not ask them to guess.

Then play the section again for the whole class to compare and check their answers.

Answers
America
England ✔
France
Brazil
Italy ✔
Japan
Spain ✔
Turkey

Younger learners
Use this as an opportunity for some real cross-curricular teaching. If you have a large map of the world, pin it up. Discuss where the countries mentioned are located and make labels in English to stick on the map.

Watch episode one again.

While you watch

Tell the class to watch the episode again very closely and to look for the objects.

1 What can you see in episode one? Tick (✔) the boxes.

This is an observation activity and is open to discussion. Give the students some time to compare their answers in pairs before discussing as a class.

Read all the words aloud with the class. Practise the words chorally and individually around the class to check pronunciation. Then ask, e.g. *Is there a globe?* Invite the class to answer *Yes, there is* or *No, there isn't*. After a couple of examples ask volunteers around the class to ask about other objects in the same way, choosing a classmate to answer.

Higher levels
Encourage higher levels to discuss and compare their answers in groups using the structures:
There's a … There isn't a… and the question form *Is there a …?*

Watch all of episode one again and check.

Go back through the episode to check the answers. You can do this at normal speed or by cueing across the video heads (speeded-up picture).

Practice

1 Can you remember?

This is a memory game. Demonstrate with known objects at the front of the class. Place about eight objects on a table at the front of the class. Ask a volunteer to come to the front, look at the objects for a few seconds and then look away or close his / her eyes. You could even use a blindfold. The volunteer should now try to remember all the objects by asking the rest of the class questions with the structure *Is there a …?* The class answer *Yes, there is* or *No, there isn't* until all the objects have been named.

The class can now play the game using the picture on Student's Book page 8. Student A looks at the picture for a few seconds only then closes the book. He / She then asks Student B *Is there a …?* questions until all eight objects have been named.

2 Chant

Practise the chant together as a class. Read Group A's line followed by Group B's response. Then divide the class into two groups with each group reading their lines in turn. Maintain a steady rhythm so that everyone is chanting in time. If possible, click your fingers twice then clap your hands twice, always with an even rhythm. Group A then join in with their lines on the clicks, and Group B answer on the claps. Begin slowly, gradually increasing the pace to make it more fun.

Higher levels
Students can practise in small groups
with two or three students reading each
set of lines. Encourage them to do so as
quickly as they can. The groups can
then perform their chants to the class,
who vote on the best one.

3 Make conversations.

Point to each of the pictures in turn and ask
Where's this?

Answers
England
France
Italy
Spain
The Moon

Use the example exchange between Wallace
and Gromit as a model for the class to repeat
as necessary. Invite pairs of volunteers from
around the class to have similar exchanges
about the other pictures,

e.g.

Student A: Let's go to England.
Student B: OK, let's go.

Higher levels
Students give other ways of suggesting
and develop the exchanges into longer
dialogues, sometimes agreeing and
sometimes disagreeing with their
partner's idea for a holiday.
e.g.
Student A: *What about going to England?*
Student B: *No. It's too wet!*

4 What's Wallace saying?

Answers
Let's have a cup of tea.
Let's have a bit of cheese.
Let's have some crackers.
Let's have a holiday.

Ask the class to tell you what Wallace is
saying for each example. Then practise
together, chorally and individually around
the class. Make sure the class understand that
all these examples use the verb 'have' whereas
in the previous activity they practised the
same expression *Let's* ... with the verb 'go'.

5 Make sentences.

On their own or in pairs the students can now
make other sentences using *Let's go to* ... and
Let's have ... .

Ask volunteers to read out some of their
suggestions to their classmates.

Higher levels
Students make sentences using as many
different ways of making suggestions as
they can,
e.g.
Shall we ...
What about ...
We could ...
Let's ...

See Student's Book page 10

11

Episode 2

The spaceship

Before you watch

1 Ask and answer.

Tell the class to look at Student's Book page 11. Point to each of the objects and ask *What's this?* Read aloud Wallace's question and Gromit's answers. Practise around the class. In pairs, tell the students to look at what's on their desk and then ask and answer each other using questions with *Have you got a ...?*

> **Higher levels**
> **Students with a wider range of vocabulary can brainstorm other things on their tables.**

Before watching the second episode, ask the class to remind you what happened in episode one. Use questions to guide them. Remind the students of the different holiday types you discussed. Divide the class into groups, give each one a different holiday, and tell them to choose ten things to pack. Compare the answers.

Ask the class where Wallace and Gromit are going on holiday. Ask the class to suggest what they will need for the journey. Pre-teach the word *spaceship* and ask volunteers to suggest how Wallace is going to get a spaceship.

Watch all of episode two.

After you watch

After watching all of episode two, ask the class if they can remember any of the tools that Wallace and Gromit used to build their

spaceship: *a saw, a hammer, a drill, a paintbrush*. Low level students will probably answer in L1. This is fine. Accept their answers, then repeat in English. Practise around the class.

2 Make sentences.

Hold up the Student's Book and point to the pictures on page 11. Point to each of the objects and ask *What's this?* Point to the pencil and ask *Who has got a pencil? Wallace or Gromit?* Encourage the students to answer with a full sentence using the prompt in the book, i.e. *Wallace has got a pencil.* Students can now write sentences about the other objects.

Answers
a pencil – Wallace
a book – Gromit
a saw – Wallace
a hammer – Wallace and Gromit
a drill – Gromit
a paintbrush – Wallace
an umbrella – Gromit

Replay episode two for students to check their answers if necessary.

3 Ask and answer.

In pairs students should now compare their answers. Demonstrate with a couple of example questions, e.g. *Has Gromit got a pencil? Has Wallace got a book?*

> **Higher levels**
> **With higher levels use activities 2 and 3 as a paired viewing activity. Send half of the class out of the room to try and write the sentences from memory. Meanwhile, the other**

Up in the Air

Flight is one of the oldest human dreams. Ancient mythology shows how people wanted to fly with the birds. On his deathbed in 1519, the genius Leonardo da Vinci said he wished he had been able to fly.

Through the years, many people tried to fly. Some came closer than others. Yet controlled flight remained a dream. Then in 1903, Wilbur and Orville Wright made their first successful flight.

Now planes fly around the world every day. But to fly alone, like a bird, is still beyond our reach. But nothing can stop the human spirit. Our ability to create new technology will join with our imaginations. New types of transportation that we cannot imagine today will be created. If people can dream it, they will learn how to build it.

As technology develops, underwater dives are not only about diving deeply. Scientists consider how long a vessel can stay beneath the water. They set goals for what a dive team can accomplish while aboard. The *Jialong* is a Chinese deep-diving submarine. It is named after a mythical sea dragon. The vessel is designed to reach depths of about 7 kilometers (4 miles/21,120 feet).

The first attempt to reach the bottom of the ocean was made in the unpowered *Bathysphere*. American engineer, Otis Barton, built it. In 1932, he and naturalist William Beebe successfully reached a depth of 923 meters (3,028 feet) in the *Bathysphere*.

Swiss scientist Auguste Piccard along with his son, Jacques, created the bathyscaphe *Trieste*. The Challenger Deep of the Mariana Trench in the Pacific Ocean is the deepest point on Earth. In 1960, Jacques and U.S. Navy Lt. Don Walsh descended into the Trench. They touched bottom at 10,915 meters (35,810 feet).

The robot *Nereus*, named for the Greek sea god, made an extremely deep dive. It submerged to 10,902 meters (35,768 feet) below the surface. People on a ship remotely controlled it.

half of the class watch the episode again, this time with no sound, and make a note of who has each of the tools. Pair off all the students so that in each pair there is a student who didn't see the episode again and one who did. Those that went outside can now ask their partner the questions to check their answers.

Walace eating crackers
Wallace drawing on the paper ✔
Wallace saying 'Vrmmm!' ✔

Higher levels
Use this opportunity to brainstorm other verbs for everyday sounds. Ask the class to close their eyes and simply listen to the sounds around them for a minute or so then describe the sounds they heard to their partner.

SECTION ONE 00.00 TO 01.33

Before you watch

1 Say these noises aloud. Then match the noises to the pictures.

Say the words so that they demonstrate the noises they are describing. For example, say *squeak ... squeak* in a very high pitched voice, say the words *drip ... drip* quickly but with a long pause before the next one. Encourage the class to do the same, then practise in pairs.

The students can then match the words to the pictures below.

While you watch

2 Tick (✔) the noises you hear.

Read the descriptions of each of the noises with the class and make sure they understand them. Encourage the class to predict which ones they are going to hear.

Watch section one.

Alternatively, you could cover the television screen so that the students are concentrating on the sound track alone.

Answers
water dripping ✔
a mouse sniffing ✔
a door creaking ✔
Wallace coming down the stairs ✔
a clock ticking
mice squeaking ✔
a light switch clicking ✔
Wallace sharpening a pencil ✔

After you watch

3 Which one can you see?

Tell the class to look at the picture of Wallace on Student's Book page 12. Ask *What is Wallace doing?* If necessary, explain that *He is playing noughts and crosses.* Noughts and crosses ('Tick, tack, toe' in American English) is a simple pen and paper game in which two players take it in turns to draw an 'O' or an 'X' in one of the nine squares on the grid. The first player to get three 'O's or 'X's in a row, wins the game. Ask the class which of the three drawings is the same as the one on the video. Have a vote on it. Then watch the section again to check.

Answer
two

Higher levels
Use this section of the video for the students to test each other's observational skills. Divide the class into groups. Watch the section (or the episode) again and tell the groups to write five observation questions for another group to answer. Swap questions then watch the section / episode again for the groups to check their answers.

13

SECTION TWO 01.33 TO THE END

Before you watch

1 Complete the spaces.

Students complete the phrases by writing the plural in the spaces.

Answers
Two mice.
Three holes.

This activity deals with irregular and regular plurals. You can use it to introduce other plurals. Choose a list of words the students are likely to know, some with regular and some with irregular plurals. Write the singular forms on the board, or dictate them to the class, and ask the students to write the correct plural for each one, e.g.:

man → men

dog → dogs

woman → women

child → children

paintbrush → paintbrushes

umbrella → umbrellas

person → people

house → houses

Watch section two.

As they watch section two, tell the class to look out for all the tools that Wallace and Gromit use to build their spaceship. Remind them of the vocabulary they learned in the previous episode.

After you watch

2 Write the sentences on the correct pictures.

Explain the meaning of each phrase to the class if necessary. Use mime and facial expressions to help demonstrate the meaning. Invite the students to describe situations in which you might use each of the phrases.

The students can now work on their own or in pairs to match the phrases to each of the pictures below.

Answers
1 Be careful!
2 Don't move, Gromit!
3 Hold on, Gromit!
4 Sorry!
5 Well done, Gromit.

If there is time, watch the section again. Ask the class to put up their hand whenever they hear one of the phrases above. Play back each phrase and practise it together, paying particular attention to Wallace's intonation.

3 Complete the sentences.

This section focuses on the Present continuous. You can use almost any video sequence to practise the Present continuous by pausing at intervals and describing what is happening or by asking *What's happening now?*

Higher levels
With higher levels, a fun way of practising the Present continuous is to arrange the class so that only some of the students can see the video. Play the sequence with the sound off and ask the viewers to describe to their classmates what is happening. The rest of the class then try to re-tell what happened.
Begin by presenting each of the verbs in turn. Use mime and say, for example, *I'm sawing.*
Repeat the mimes but this time say *I'm ...* and pause for the students to provide the correct participle. At this point make sure the students are stressing the first syllable, e.g. <u>dri</u>lling, <u>whist</u>ling, <u>rea</u>ding, etc. Now read the words in the box together before asking the class to use them to complete the sentences.
You may need to explain *welding* – joining pieces of metal together by hammering or pressing them, usually when the metal is hot. A person who does this as a job is called *a welder.*

Answers
1 Gromit is reading a book.
2 Wallace is sawing.
3 Wallace is whistling.
4 Gromit is hammering a nail.
5 Gromit is drilling a hole.
6 Gromit is welding.
7 Wallace is painting the spaceship.

4 Ask and answer.

Demonstrate the activity. Point to each picture in turn and ask *What's he doing?* Encourage the students to answer with a full sentence, e.g. *He's reading a book.* Ask volunteers from around the class to choose a classmate and to ask him / her the same question about a different picture. The students then practise the question and answers in pairs.

If time, play the episode again. Pause at intervals and ask *What's Wallace / Gromit doing?*

Watch episode two again.

Practice

1 Match the spaceships to the colours.

This activity practises colour words. For most students this should be revision. With lower levels, point to each spaceship in turn and ask *What colour is this?* Review the colour words if necessary. Then ask randomly around the class, e.g. *What colour is number seven?* If you have time, make this a memory game. Ask similar questions, but this time the students answer with their books closed. If you want to add a competitive element, divide the class into two teams and give a point for every correct answer.

Answers

1	orange	6	pink
2	blue	7	grey
3	green	8	black
4	yellow	9	white
5	red	10	brown

Higher levels
Brainstorm other colour words with the class. Alternatively, put the class into groups, set a time limit and ask them to write down as many colour words as they can. Other colour words might include: *purple, (lilac, violet), cream, beige, turquoise, maroon, silver, gold.*

Ask and answer about things in the classroom.

Model the question by reading Wallace and Gromit's speech bubbles. Ask other example questions with *What colour's your / the …?* around the class, then encourage volunteers to ask their classmates in the same way. Students can then practise in pairs.

2 Chant

Practise the chant together as a class. Read Group A's line followed by Group B's sound words. Then divide the class into two groups with each group reading their lines in turn. Make sure you maintain a steady rhythm so that everyone is chanting in time. If possible, click your fingers twice then clap your hands twice, always with an even rhythm. Group A then join in with their lines on the clicks, and Group B answer on the claps. Begin slowly, gradually increasing the pace to make it more fun!

Higher levels
Students write their own 'sounds' chant or poem following the model in the Student's Book. Encourage them to vary the verbs and sounds as much as possible.

3 Find these pets in the picture.

Explain the meaning of the word *pet.* Ask the class if anyone has a pet. Read the words in the box with the class. Explain any unknown words using board drawings or the picture on Student's Book page 16. Tell the class to repeat the words after you chorally and then individually. Check for correct pronunciation.

In pairs the students can now look for all the pets in the picture.

15

Note: In Britain many families have a pet. This is usually a dog or a cat, but many families keep other animals in their homes such as *mice*, *hamsters*, *fish*, and *birds*, such as *budgerigars*. Some schools even have class pets.

Young learners
Make a 'Pet corner' for your classroom. Ask the children to bring in soft toy animals they have at home. Use the animals to teach animal names in English and to talk about the animals: describe them, discuss what they eat and how you would look after them if they were real pets.

Answers

a cat – on the back of the armchair
a hamster – in the wheel, on the table
a dog – Gromit, standing by the door
a rabbit – under the table
a mouse – in the hole, by the door
a bird – on the lamp
a fish – in a bowl, on the sideboard

Higher levels
Students describe to you the exact location of each of the pets.

Match the questions to the answers.

With lower levels go through the activity orally with the whole class before asking the students to match and copy the questions and answers into their note books.

Higher levels
Students match and write the questions and answers straight into their notebooks. If you are confident with pronunciation, you could spend some time comparing the falling intonation in 'Wh' questions with the rising intonation at the end of 'Yes / No' questions, e.g.

Have you got a pet?

What's its name?

Note: 'its' is the demonstrative adjective and not 'it's', which is short for *it is*.

Answers
1 C
2 D
3 E
4 A
5 B

Ask and answer about your pets.

Divide the class into groups so that in each group there is at least one student who has a pet. The rest of the group find out about the pet using the questions in the Student's Book.
Note: they can invent a pet if necessary.

Higher levels
Encourage students to produce at least five other questions to make the interview more interesting, e.g.
How long have you had your pet?
Who gave it to you?
What does it eat?
Where does it sleep?
What does it look like?

4 Give and follow instructions.

Read the speech bubbles with the class. Ask the students to suggest situations where you might use or hear these commands. Can they remember which of the phrases they heard in Episode 2?

Say the instructions and ask the class to do what you tell them. The students can then practise in pairs.

Higher levels:
Much higher level students work in pairs or small groups to write a short dialogue or story in which they include as many of the commands as possible. Invite volunteers to read out their stories / dialogues to the rest of the class.

See Student's Book page 17

Episode 3
Blast off!

Watching the video.

Before you watch

1 Put the numbers in words.

Note: 'Blast off!' is the expression used when a rocket or spaceship takes off from a launching site. You will usually hear it, as here, at the end of a countdown: '10, 9, 8, 7, 6, 5, 4, 3, 2, 1, Blast off!'.

Ask the class to suggest why this is the title for this episode. How does it help them to guess what is going to happen?

Quickly review the numbers one to ten orally with the class. Write the numbers on the board one at a time as you say them with the class.

The students can now match the words to the numbers on Student's Book page 18.

Answers

ten   nine   eight   seven   six
five   four   three   two   one

Practise counting backwards and forwards. Make this into a fun game by asking the students to count around the class with each student saying a number. Begin by counting forwards then when you clap your hands, the next student has to continue counting but now backwards. Continue with a few more students then change direction again.

> **Higher levels**
> Practise with more difficult combinations, e.g.
> 2 4 6 8 10 ...
> and
> 1 3 5 7 9 ...

> **Younger learners**
> Tell the children they are going to be a spaceship. Tell everyone to crouch down on the floor and count down together: 10, 9, 8 ... On 'Blast off!' everyone jumps into the air.

Watch all of episode three.

Before watching, ask the class a simple question to focus on the general meaning of the episode, e.g. *What does Wallace forget?*

Note: In Britain crackers are traditionally eaten with cheese. Wallace is a traditionalist, and it is important for him to go to the Moon with a good supply of crackers. Although there are a variety of crackers available, the type shown here in the orange and black packaging are the traditional crackers which are very popular in Britain.

After you watch

2 Label the pictures.

Read the words with the class. In pairs students then try to match as many words as they know. Check their answers and teach any new words using the pictures to help you.

Answers

1 fuse
2 suitcase
3 controls
4 match
5 ladder
6 clock
7 brake

Higher levels
Ask the students to put each word into
a sentence that illustrates its meaning.

SECTION ONE 00.00 TO 01.16

Before you watch

1 Complete the spaces.

Present the prepositions *into*, *up* and *down*
using the pictures on Student's Book page
19. Hold up your book and point to each
picture in turn asking *Where is Wallace
going?* The students can then practise the
phrases in pairs or write them in their books.

Answers
down the stairs
up the ladder
into the spaceship
down the ladder
up the ladder again

Higher levels
Students invent other sentences, or a
short story, using the three prepositions.
Alternatively, you could discuss other
prepositions, e.g. *along, out of,
through, between*, etc. and the students
use them to describe an unusual
journey.

Watch section one.

After you watch

2 Match the sentences to the pictures.

This activity reviews and contextualizes some
of the vocabulary presented on Student's
Book page 18. Encourage the students to
match each sentence to one of the pictures
using these known words as clues. Replay the
section as necessary pausing at the
appropriate frames.

Answers
2 3 4 1

Note the expression to 'strike a match',
meaning to light a match. Traditionally,
matches in Britain were made by a company
called 'Swan Vesta' who always use a picture
of a swan on the matchbox. If you look
carefully at Wallace's matches, you will see
how the makers of the video have made a
joke of this by putting a duck on the
traditional box instead.

SECTION TWO 01.16 TO THE END

Before you watch

1 Number the pictures in order from 1 to 7.

Tell the class to look at the pictures on
Student's Book page 20 and to number the
pictures in the correct order. Put the students
into pairs to compare their answers. At this
stage tell them not to worry if they are not
sure about the exact order.

While you watch

Watch section two and check.

Replay section two for the class to check
their answers. You may need to do this more
than once, pausing if necessary.

Answers
4 3 7 2 6 5 1

After you watch

2 Match the sentences to the pictures.

Ask volunteers to read each of the sentences.
Check understanding and teach / review the
language as necessary. In pairs, the students
can now match each sentence to the correct
picture above.

Ask members of the class to read out the
sentences in the correct order. Alternatively,

you could ask the whole class to write the sentences in order.

Answers
Wallace is coming down the stairs. 5
Gromit is waiting for Wallace. 4
They're going to the Moon. 7
What are you looking for, Wallace? 2
Wallace is closing the door. 6
The doors are opening. 1
Wallace is getting the crackers. 3

Higher levels
Ask the students to use the pictures and the sentences as a framework to help them re-write an account of Section two in the past. Encourage them to use connectors, conjunctions, etc. to make the narrative flow. Invite volunteers to read out their accounts to the rest of the class.

Before you watch again

3 Complete Wallace's sentences.

Tell the class to complete each of Wallace's speech bubbles, either from memory or using contextual clues in the pictures to help them guess the missing words. (There is only one word missing in all cases except one.) Compare students' answers and discuss different possibilities. At this stage accept what is linguistically correct. Don't insist on what Wallace actually says on the video.

While you watch

4 Watch and check.

Play section two again for the class to check their answers. Encourage the students to tell you when to 'stop' the video. Pause / rewind as necessary to focus on the language.

Answers

Let me see.
We're ready now.
Sixty seconds to blast off.
We haven't got the crackers.
Wait for me, Gromit.

Watch episode three again.

Practice

This section practises numbers up to *one hundred* and focuses on the structure *How many ...?* For higher levels you could extend the work to include *hundreds* and *thousands*. Write some digits on the board and ask the students to read out the numbers or to write them in word form,

e.g.

4, 562 = *four thousand, five hundred and sixty-two.*

127, 983 = *one hundred and twenty-seven thousand, nine hundred and eighty-three.*

Note that in English, in this situation, we do not use the plural of *hundred* or *thousand* and that thousands are separated by a comma in five figure numbers plus, e.g. 10,000 (but 1000) .

1 Put the numbers on the clock.

Students write the number words under / next to the corresponding digits on the clock face.

Answers
10 – ten
15 – fifteen
20 – twenty
25 – twenty-five
30 – thirty
35 – thirty-five
40 – forty
45 – forty-five
50 – fifty
55 – fifty-five
60 – sixty

Spend a little time focusing on the pronunciation of, e.g. *fifteen* and *fifty* as even very fluent students find this difficult. Note that in *fifteen* it is the second syllable which is stressed: *fifteen* and is pronounced with a long /iː/. When we say *fifty,* we stress the first syllable: *fifty* so that the 'y' is pronounced as a short /ɪ/ sound. The same applies to all other '-een' and '-y' numbers, e.g. *eighteen* and *eighty*. If your students find this difficult, practise with some minimal pair-work. Do a simple numbers dictation in which you randomly say a list of '-een' and '-y' numbers. The students listen and write down the digits. Students can then practise this in pairs.

19

2 Say these numbers aloud.

Practise saying the numbers, paying particular attention to the stress. Note that when we say, for example, *fifty-nine, forty-five, thirty-three*, etc. the stress is always on the second part.

3 Find the numbers.

Students can do the word search puzzle on their own or in pairs by finding the words for the digits in the box.

Answers

As a possible extension students could make their own number word-search puzzles using square paper for their partner to solve.

4 Chant

The chant recycles in a fun way some of the language the students have been practising in this episode. Say each line for the class to repeat after you, reviewing the vocabulary if necessary. Explain that *hatch* is a small door in a boat, ship, spacecraft, aircraft, etc.

Encourage the class to chant the words rhythmically. If possible, get the class to click their fingers or clap their hands to maintain a steady beat.

5 Ask and answer.

If necessary, do this as a whole class activity first. Read the questions for students around the class to answer. Explain the meaning of any new vocabulary, e.g. *sunglasses, tins (of paint), shelves.*

Students should then ask each other in pairs. Student A asks the first set of questions for Student B to answer and Student B asks the second set of questions for Student A to answer.

Answers

How many mice are there?   Ten
How many yellow sunglasses are there?   Two
How many white sunglasses are there?   Four
How many pink sunglasses are there?   Two
How many blue sunglasses are there?   One
How many green sunglasses are there?   One

How many tins of paint are there?   Eight
How many shelves are there?   Two
How many tins are on the bottom shelf?   Six
How many tins are on the top shelf?   Two

See Student's Book page 26

Watching the video

Before you watch

1 Ask and answer.

Model the question and two possible answers by reading Wallace and Gromit's speech bubbles. Then ask other *Do you like … ?* questions using the picture prompts on Student's Book page 25. Encourage the class to use full *Yes, I do* or *No, I don't* answers but don't insist on it as short *Yes* or *No* answers are equally correct.

Ask students from around the class to choose a classmate to ask a question to, then practise in pairs. Monitor and correct as necessary, paying particular attention to pronunciation.

> **Higher levels**
> Students make up their own questionnaires using other *Do you like …ing?* and *Do you like* + noun questions.

Watch all of episode four.

Before playing all of episode four, ask the class a general question about the story of the episode, e.g. *What do Wallace and Gromit do on the Moon?*

After you watch

2 Tick (✔) the correct sentences.

This activity compares simple affirmative and negative structures and recycles some of the vocabulary from the previous activity. Read

the four pairs of sentences with the class using the pictures in the Student's Book or mime to reinforce the meaning. The students then choose the correct sentence in each example. Put the students into pairs to read and compare their answers.

Answers
The toast is hot.
You can't play football on the Moon.
The Moon is made of cheese.
Wallace likes picnics.

> **Higher levels**
> Students work in pairs or small groups to write other pairs of sentences, one affirmative and one negative. These could be sentences about Wallace and Gromit and '*A Grand Day Out*'™ so far, or they could be more general facts in the form of a general knowledge quiz. Groups / pairs of students can then swap sentences.

> **Higher levels**
> With higher level students discuss why you can't play football on the Moon. (There is not enough gravity on the Moon.)

21

Before you watch

1 Number the pictures in order from 1 to 7.

Hold up your Student's Book, point to the set of pictures and ask *What's Gromit doing?* Tell the class to look at the pictures carefully and order them by numbering each one from 1 to 7. In pairs, the class compare their answers before checking as a class.

Answers

2	5	7	
1	3	6	4

2 Count the cards in each picture.

Using the pictures on Student's Book page 26 again, and the answers from the previous activity, tell the class to count how many cards there are in each picture. Do this individually then compare answers in pairs before discussing together as a class. Ask students around the class, e.g. *How many cards are there in picture number (one)?*

Answers

Picture number	1	2	3	4	5	6	7
How many cards?	2	6	10	10	21	26	26

Watch section one.

After you watch

3 Tick (✔) the correct answers.

This activity practises 'Yes / No' questions and short answers. Go through each of the questions with the class, explaining the meaning where necessary. Tell the class to work on their own to tick the correct answers. Any answers they are not sure about they should guess or leave blank. In pairs students compare their answers. Encourage one student to read the questions and the other to read his / her selected answer. Then swap roles so that everyone has the opportunity to practise both questions and

answers. If necessary, repeat the section for everyone to check their answers.

Answers

1 Yes, it is.
2 Yes, he has.
3 No, he isn't.
4 Yes, he has.
5 Yes, it is.

Higher levels
Extend the language to review other 'Yes / No' questions and short answers. Write a series of answers on the board, e.g.
No, I didn't.
Yes, she did.
No, I won't.
Yes, I could.
No, we wouldn't.
Yes, you should.
Now tell the students to write a possible question for each answer, but in a jumbled order. The class then exchange questions and choose the correct answer from the board.

Before you watch

1 Label the picture.

Read the words in the box with the class, paying particular attention to pronunciation. Students then label the picture before comparing with a partner.

Higher levels
Students use the words in the box to write a detailed description of the scene.

Answers

basket saucer
apple cup
bag
Thermos flask
sugar tablecloth cheese

While you watch

2 What has Wallace got in his bag?

Ask the class if they can remember what Gromit has in his bag.

Watch section two and check.

Answer
A plate, a knife and some crackers.

After you watch

3 Write the sentences on the correct picture.

Practise each of the expressions with the class, explaining the meaning if necessary. Then tell the students to match each sentence to one of the pictures. Students can compare their answers with a partner before watching the section again to check their answers.

Answers
(from left to right)
What kind is it?
You try it.
I don't know, lad.

4 Say the cheese names aloud.

Cultural note:
Wensleydale, Stilton and Cheddar are three of the most popular English cheeses.

Wensleydale is a mild, white, crumbly cheese. It is made in Yorkshire where the Wallace and Gromit videos are set, which is probably why it is Wallace's favourite!

Stilton is a blue-veined, hard cheese. It is traditionally eaten at Christmas time.

Cheddar is a hard cheese from the south-west of England and is the most common English cheese.

Gorgonzola is a rich creamy blue-veined Italian cheese.

Note that the cheese names have been broken down into syllables. Say each cheese name several times and see if the class can identify which syllable is stressed:

● ● ●   ● ●
Wensleydale   Stilton

● ●   ● ● ●
Cheddar   Gorgonzola

Practise saying the cheese names with the class. See if the class know any more cheese names, either from England or elsewhere.

Watch episode four again.

After you watch

1 What's happening in the pictures?

This activity reviews the main events in the story and focuses on the Present continuous tense. Go through each of the pictures orally with the class. For each picture ask *What's happening in picture (one)?*

Answers
1 Wallace is reading a newspaper.
2 Gromit is building a house of cards.
3 Wallace is taking a photo.
4 Wallace is eating toast.
5 Wallace and Gromit are walking on the Moon.
6 Wallace is drinking tea.
7 Wallace is cutting the cheese.
8 Wallace is eating cheese.
9 Gromit is sniffing the cheese.

Higher levels
Higher level students write down the answers. Use this activity to explain the following spelling rules:
1) If a verb ends in 'e', we drop it before adding ' -ing', e.g. *take →* *taking, bite → biting, rise → rising.* **(There are exceptions to this rule, but students are unlikely to come across them at this level.)**
2) When the (last) syllable has a short vowel sound followed by a single consonant, e.g. *cut, begin,* **we double the final consonant, i.e.** *cutting, beginning.*
Tell the class to write the *-ing* **forms of some other verbs, e.g.:**
hide, sit, drive, put, make, go, sleep, run, **etc.**

23

Practice

1 Mime game

Demonstrate the game. Choose an action to mime and ask *What am I doing?* Whoever guesses correctly can then come to the front and do a different mime from the list. When you are happy that everyone understands the activity and has had sufficient practice of both the question and answer, the class can continue playing the game in pairs.

Higher levels
Divide the class into teams. Tell each team to write a list of actions on a piece of paper. Take in all the lists. Choose a volunteer and give him / her a mime from another team's list of actions. Set a time limit for the rest of the team to name the action. Repeat with a volunteer from each team in turn and award a point for every correctly guessed mime.

2 Chant

Say each line for the class to repeat after you, reviewing / teaching the vocabulary if necessary, using the picture on Student's Book page 29.

Encourage the class to chant the words rhythmically and with the correct stress.

3 Tick (✔) the correct spelling.

This is a good opportunity to practise using monolingual or bilingual dictionaries if the students have them. Say each of the words aloud and tell the students to look at the four different spellings. Explain that in each case only one spelling is correct. Once they have completed the activity, students can compare their choices in pairs.

Answers
knife
toast
bored
ready
brake
happening
reading
walking

4 Match the opposites.

Read the words aloud with the class, then tell them to match each word on the left hand side with one of the words on the right. Compare answers in pairs before checking as a whole class.

Answers
up – down
quickly – slowly
hot – cold
on – off
in – out

Higher levels
Use this opportunity to review other adjectives, adverbs and prepositions. Call out the words for the class to say the opposites. You could do this as a whole class or individually around the class. Do this activity quickly, having prepared a list of words beforehand.

5 Ask your partner to do these things.

Practise the commands with the whole class, demonstrating the actions yourself if necessary. Students can then practise in pairs.

Higher levels
Choose a few verbs. Make them as varied as possible, e.g. *eat an orange, read a book, sing a song, drive a car,* etc. Tell the class to choose as many adverbs as they can think of to describe different ways in which you might do the actions. Ask volunteers to use their adverbs to give commands to the rest of the class, e.g. *Eat an orange carefully; Drive a car fast.* The rest of the class then try to mime the action in the appropriate manner.

Transcript

See Student's Book page 31

The Moon machine

Watching the video

Before you watch

1 What can you buy?

Point to the pictures on page 32 of the Student's Book and ask *What are these?* Teach the word *slot machines*.

Note: *slot* is the thin hole where you put the coins in machines like the ones shown on Student's Book page 32. The modern term for *slot machine* is 'vending machine'. These usually sell small items such as chocolate bars, drinks and sometimes tickets.

Ask the class to tell you what you can buy from each of the machines.

Answers
chocolate
cold drinks
train tickets

In pairs ask the class to make a list of other things they can buy from slot machines in their town. Use the model in Wallace and Gromit's speech bubbles to practise the question and answer around the class. Students can then practise in pairs.

> **Higher levels**
> Students work individually or in pairs to invent and design their own slot machines. They can then write step by step instructions on how to use their machines and read them out to the class.

Watch all of episode five.

Ask the class to predict what sort of slot machine they think Wallace and Gromit are going to find on the Moon.

After you watch

2 Make sentences about the pictures with the words from the box.

Read the verbs in the box then use the example to model a sentence about the machine using *can*. Ask volunteers around the class to make similar sentences about the other pictures, choosing from the verbs in the box.

Answers
It can see.
It can move.
It can ski.
It can read.
It can write.

Ask questions around the class with *Can it...?* Use the verbs in the box then encourage the class to ask and answer different questions with other verbs, e.g. *Can it hear? Can it speak?*

In most British towns and cities, streets have parking metres or ticket machines where you buy a ticket to park your vehicle for a period of time. At regular intervals traffic wardens patrol the streets, giving heavy fines to people whose tickets have expired. They are not generally very popular. The Moon machine is both a ticket machine and a traffic warden.

SECTION ONE 00.00 TO 02.10

Before you watch

1 Label the picture.

Read the words and practise with the class before they label the pictures individually, then compare with their partners.

Note that the word *drawer* is pronounced in the same way as the verb *draw (a picture)*.

Answers

control   antenna
slot   eye
wheel   arm
drawer   hand

2 Answer the questions.

Ask two students to read the example question and answer. Correct the pronunciation and practise with the whole class, if necessary, using a simple substitution drill:

Teacher: *How many controls has it got?*
Students: *How many controls has it got?*
Teacher: *wheels*
Students: *How many wheels has it got?*
Teacher: *hands*
Students: *How many hands has it got?*
etc.

Answers

It's got four controls.
It's got three wheels.
It's got two hands.
It's got one eye.

Watch section one.

After you watch

3 Match the sentences to the pictures.

Read each of the sentences with the class teaching / reviewing vocabulary as necessary.

Note that here the expression *the rest* means *the rest of (all the other) crockery and cutlery* (plates, cups, knives, etc.).

Answers
4 2 5 3 1

4 Tick (✔) the correct answers.

Go through each of the questions with the class explaining any new language, e.g. *broken, alive, telescope.* Students should then choose the correct answer and check with their partner before discussing the answers as a class.

Answers
1 No, it isn't.
2 Yes, it is.
3 Yes, it has.
4 Yes, it can.

> **Higher levels**
> Students make other questions about the machine beginning:
> *Is it ...?*
> *Has it got ...?*
> *Can it ...?*
> Students then read out their questions for their classmates to answer.

> **Higher levels**
> Have a class discussion entitled 'What makes you angry?' Encourage the class to discuss the things that anger them. Begin the discussion by giving examples for yourself, e.g.:
> *People who drop litter make me angry.*
> *Noizy people make me angry!*
> *Long queues in the supermarket make me angry.*

> **Young learners**
> With younger children you might want to talk about what makes their parents or teachers angry – and why. You may need to do this in the children's own language.

SECTION TWO 2.10 TO THE END

Before you watch

1 Match the sentences to the pictures.

Use mime to present the adjectives *hurt*, *angry* and *surprised*. Then call out an adjective and tell the class to mime the emotion. Repeat for each of the three adjectives.

The students can then match each adjective to the correct picture.

Answers
3 2 1

Watch section two.

After you watch

2 Make sentences.

Use the example to model the expression *It's angry about the ...* Then ask the class to make similar sentences about the other pictures.

Answers
It's angry about the oil leak.
It's angry about the cheese.
It's angry about the spaceship.
It's angry about the picnic.

3 Ask and answer about the pictures.

Before practising the question and answer, make sure the class understand the difference between *What's this?* and *What's that?*

Read each of the words in the box, paying particular attention to pronunciation. Invite the class to ask you *What's that?* for each of the pictures. Answer with *It's (glue)*. Then you ask the questions for the class to answer. Finally, the students can ask and answer each other in pairs.

Note that the word *glue* is uncountable and doesn't have an article. Also that a *truncheon* is usually used by a policeman. Here it is a symbol of the Moon machine's authority.

Answers
It's glue.
It's a notebook.
It's a parking ticket.
It's a truncheon.

4 Make a list.

Quickly review all the vocabulary using the pictures on Student's Book page 35. Ask students to list all the items they think the machine has got in its drawer at the end of the episode.

Watch episode five again and check.

5 Ask and answer.

After watching the whole episode again to check their answers, students compare their answers by asking each other in pairs about each of the objects. Demonstrate and practise both the question and possible answers. Use Wallace and Gromit's models if necessary.

Answer

The objects in the machine's drawer at the end of the episode are:

a telescope
a cup
a saucer
a plate
a knife
a holiday / ski magazine
glue
a notebook
a pencil

Practice

1 Can you do it?
Ask your partner.

Demonstrate the activity using Wallace and Gromit's model dialogue on Student's Book page 36. Read the speech bubbles together. Then do the same for the other questions, asking a different student each time. Students can then practise in pairs.

Higher levels

Students think up other questions with *Can you ...?* If you particularly want to focus on adverbs, you could insist that every question uses a different adverb:

Can you whistle loudly?
Can you say the alphabet backwards?

Young learners

With young learners a fun way to practise adverbs is to use a well-known song. Invite the class to sing the song in the normal way. On pieces of paper write some adverbs for different ways in which the children can sing the song, e.g. *slowly, quickly, loudly, quietly, sadly, angrily*, etc. Invite the children to sing the song again. This time, hold up a card, e.g. 'quickly' and demonstrate to the children how they should speed up their singing. Repeat with the other adverbs. When the children understand the activity, hold up different cards randomly. Then divide the class into groups. Give each group a different card to practise singing a verse in that particular way.

2 Chant

Build up the chant gradually. Say the first line and ask the class to repeat after you. Then say the first and second lines and again ask the class to repeat. Do the same with the first three lines and so on, until the class are repeating the whole chant after you.

Higher levels

Focus on the rhyming words and the sounds that they share. On the board write three words from the chant: *slot*, *bar* and *ball*. In pairs or groups students write as many other words as they can that rhyme with each of these three words from the chant.

3 Match the words to the pictures.

Before completing the speech bubbles, encourage the class to use the pictures to describe what is happening. Then read the five phrases and make sure the meaning of each one is clear. Ask the class to suggest when someone might say, e.g. *Ouch!* or *Be careful!*

In pairs students can then match each of the phrases to the correct picture and complete the speech bubbles.

Answers
Gromit can ski.
Be careful, Gromit!
Ouch!
Are you hurt?
That's better?

Higher levels
Tell the students that the five frames are stills from a video clip. Explain that you want them to write a short transcript to include the five phrases above as well as a narrative to describe the sequence of events as they happen. Divide the class into groups of three to write the transcript and then to act out the sequence as Wallace, Gromit and the narrator.

4 Word chain

This activity revises vocabulary from this and previous episodes. Although the focus of the activity is the spelling of the words, this is an ideal opportunity to review the meanings quickly before doing the puzzle.

Demonstrate how the puzzle works using the example. If necessary, begin another word chain on the board, this time inviting students to suggest each word.

Answer
(other combinations are possible)

antenna arm matches slot teapot
truncheon nought Thermos spaceship picnic
cupboard drill lamp photo oil ladder

Higher levels
Play a game. Begin the game by saying *Yesterday I went shopping, and I bought a saw.*

Then choose a student to continue the game by repeating your sentence but adding another item, which must begin with the last letter of your item, i.e. 'w'. For example, *Yesterday I went shopping, and I bought a saw and a watch.* **Each player continues the list of shopping items always adding a word beginning with the last letter of the previous word in the list of items bought. Anyone who makes a mistake or forgets a word is out.**

5 Find the different word.

Read the words. Students take it in turns to read a word around the class. In each set of four words there is one word which does not belong. This is called the 'odd one out'. Ask the students to find the word that is different from all the others in each of the six sets. If necessary, do the first example with the class.

Answers

notebook
knife
truncheon
cheese
hot
glue

Higher levels
Students explain each of their answers, e.g.
You read a book, a magazine and a newspaper but you write in a notebook.

Transcript

See Student's Book page 38

Back to the Earth

Watching the video

Before you watch

1 What do you want for your birthday?

Ask three students to 'be' Wallace, Gromit and the Moon machine. Ask each one the question *What do you want for your birthday?* The students read the speech bubbles in order to answer your question. Then ask other students, *What does (Wallace) want for his birthday?* Students answer using the examples in the Student's Book to help them if necessary.

In groups students can then do a quick survey of what their classmates want for their birthday. The groups then report back to the class, e.g.:

David wants a computer.

Anna wants a bike.

> **Higher levels**
> Use this as an opportunity to use reported speech. Students report back to the class on what their classmates said. Use: *He said, 'I like it.'* rather than, *He said that he liked it.*

Watch episode six.

Before watching the final episode, read the title with the class. Make sure they know what it means and ask the class to predict what is going to happen. Higher levels can do this in English, whereas lower levels might need to use some L1.

After you watch

2 Complete the sentences.

Read each of the six adjectives and practise around the class. Use mime and facial expressions to make the meaning clear. Then say the adjectives randomly for the class to mime. Students complete the sentences before comparing their answers with a partner. Repeat the episode if necessay, pausing at the relevant points so that the class can check their anwers.

Answers
Gromit is tired.
Wallace is hurt.
Wallace is scared.
The machine is sad.
The machine is angry.
The machine is happy.

> **Higher levels**
> Students continue the sentences adding *because …* and giving a reason why each of the characters feels as he does.

> **Young learners**
> Tell young learners to make themselves look angry, tired, scared, etc. Alternatively, get them to draw different faces or make masks that are clearly happy, sad, angry, etc. Encourage them to talk about what makes them happy, sad or angry.

Before you watch

1 Match the sentences with the pictures.

Talk about what is happening in each of the pictures. The students then try to match one of the sentences to each picture before comparing with a partner.

Answers

5 6 1 2 3 4

While you watch

Watch section one and check.

Students watch section one to check their answers then discuss with the whole class.

> **Higher levels**
> Students use the pictures and the sentences to write an account of what happened in section one.

Before you watch

1 Match the words.

Read through the two lists of words with the class. Quickly review the list of nouns on the bottom. If the students have forgotten *tin*, you can point out that we had *tins of paint* in episode three, and *tin-opener* in this episode.

Demonstrate the activity using the model answer. Then tell the students to match the other verbs on the top with a noun on the bottom. Students can then compare answers in pairs before checking as a whole class.

> **Lower levels**
> With lower levels, do this orally as a whole activity first.

Answers

climb a ladder
open a tin
strike a match
wave goodbye
set the controls
read a newspaper
eat cheese

> **Higher levels**
> Students think of another noun to use with each of the verbs. This would be a good opportunity for practise in using a monolingual dictionary.

Watch section two.

After you watch

2 Choose the correct words.

Depending on the level of the class, go through the activity orally with the whole class first as this is quite challenging. Alternatively, students can do the activity in pairs then discuss as a class to check their answers.

Answers

It likes skiing but it can't ski on the Moon. It hasn't got any skis. It wants to go to the Earth, because it can ski on the Earth.
It has got skis now. It can ski on the Moon. It's happy.

3 Tell the story.

Discuss each of the pictures in turn with the class. Encourage the students to cover up the words and to talk about what they can see. Use simple questions to guide them and to present or elicit any language they will need to understand the text. The students can then read the text, individually, in pairs, or as a whole class.

Higher levels
Students use the text and the pictures to re-tell the events in the past. They could do this as a letter from Wallace to a friend or perhaps as a newspaper article. Make sure the students understand that the text here has been greatly simplified, and that they will need to expand the text and use various devices to make the language flow as a narrative.

Watch section two again.

In a later lesson

Watch all of 'A Grand Day Out'.
In a later lesson, let the class watch the whole video straight through and enjoy it without any interruptions.

Practice

1 Ask and answer.
Read the questions with the class. Practise as necessary, paying particular attention to pronunciation and intonation. In pairs or small groups, students take it in turns to ask the questions and discuss the answers. Follow this up with a whole class feedback and discussion.

Higher levels
Students think up another two questions for each of the pictures. In pairs they ask and answer each other's questions before discussing with the whole class.

2 Say aloud.
Demonstrate the activity by going through each of the examples with the whole class, showing the students how to change an affirmative imperative into a negative one using *Don't ...* . Students practise in pairs, swapping roles so that all have the opportunity to practise both sets of commands.

Higher levels
Students write a list of rules for on board Wallace and Gromit's spaceship.

3 Find the word with the different sound.
This activity focuses on sounds rather than meaning. Demonstrate the activity using the model answer in the first example. Say each of the words and see if the class can tell you why the word *pen* has been circled (it has a short /e/ sound, whereas all the other words have long /i:/ sounds). If necessary, read the other sets of words with the class and see if they can identify the different sound in each group. If the students are more confident, give them the task to do individually or in pairs, then compare as a class.

Higher levels
If students are familiar with phonetic symbols, you could use them to explain the different sounds here. Alternatively, students could use a monolingual or bilingual dictionary to check their answers and write further examples for their classmates.

Answers
pen
go
run
ski
back
want

Transcript

See Student's Book page 45